Pebble® Plus

Sharks

Mako Shark

by Deborah Nuzzolo

Consulting Editor: Gail Saunders-Smith, PhD

Consultant: Jody Rake, member
Southwest Marine/Aquatic Educators' Association

Capstone press®

Mankato, Minnesota

Pebble Plus is published by Capstone Press,
1710 Roe Crest Drive, North Mankato, Minnesota 56003.
www.capstonepub.com

Copyright © 2009 by Capstone Press, a Capstone imprint. All rights reserved.
No part of this publication may be reproduced in whole or in part, or stored in a retrieval system, or transmitted
in any form or by any means, electronic, mechanical, photocopying, recording, or otherwise, without written
permission of the publisher. For information regarding permission, write to Capstone Press,
1710 Roe Crest Drive, North Mankato, Minnesota 56003.

Library of Congress Cataloging-in-Publication Data
Nuzzolo, Deborah.
    Mako shark / by Deborah Nuzzolo.
      p. cm. — (Pebble plus. Sharks)
    Includes bibliographical references and index.
    Summary: "Simple text and photographs present mako sharks, their body parts,
and their behavior" — Provided by publisher.
    ISBN-13: 978-1-4296-1729-1 (hardcover)
    ISBN-10: 1-4296-1729-2 (hardcover)
    1. Mako sharks — Juvenile literature. I. Title.
QL638.95.L3N89 2009
597.3'3 — dc22   2007051335

Editorial Credits
Megan Peterson, editor; Ted Williams, set designer; Kyle Grenz, book designer; Jo Miller, photo researcher

Photo Credits
Alamy/Stephen Frink Collection, 4–5; Visual&Written SL, cover, 9, 10–11
Bruce Coleman Inc./Maris Kazmers, 1
Corbis/Amos Nachoum, 7
Getty Images Inc./Visuals Unlimited/Richard Herrmann, 13
Nature Picture Library/Doug Perrine, 19
Seapics/Caterina Gennaro-Kurr, 16–17; Richard Herrmann, 15, 20–21
Shutterstock/Simone Conti, backgrounds

Note to Parents and Teachers

The Sharks set supports national science standards related to the characteristics and
behavior of animals. This book describes and illustrates mako sharks. The images support
early readers in understanding the text. The repetition of words and phrases helps early
readers learn new words. This book also introduces early readers to
subject-specific vocabulary words, which are defined in the Glossary section. Early
readers may need assistance to read some words and to use the Table of Contents,
Glossary, Read More, Internet Sites, and Index sections of the book.

Printed in the United States of America in North Mankato, Minnesota.
082015
009140R

Table of Contents

Fast Sharks

What is the fastest shark

in the sea?

It's the mako shark.

Mako sharks live worldwide
in warm and cool water.
They swim along the shore
and in deeper water.

7

What They Look Like

Two kinds of mako sharks
dash through the sea.
They are shortfin makos
and longfin makos.

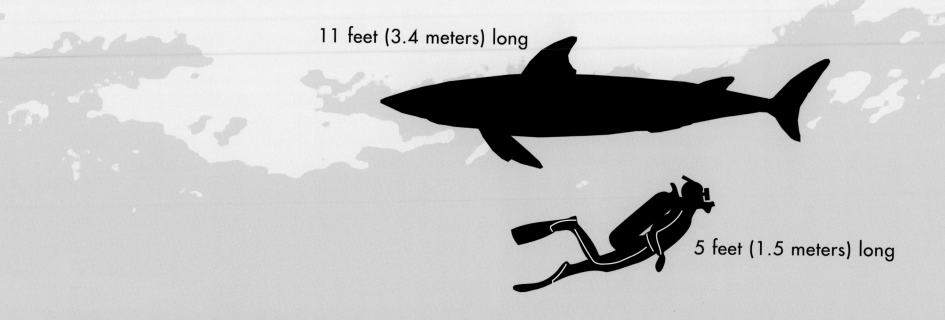

11 feet (3.4 meters) long

5 feet (1.5 meters) long

9

Shortfin makos
have shorter pectoral fins
than longfin makos.
These fins help sharks steer
like wings on an airplane.

pectoral fins

Mako sharks have
large black eyes.
They see well in dim light.

Mako Shark Pups

Mako shark eggs
hatch inside the mother.
Between four and 16 pups
are born at one time.

Hunting

Mako sharks hunt tuna, mackerel, and swordfish.

The mako shark uses
its strong tail
to zoom after prey.

Mako sharks attack
with sharp, hooklike teeth.
They are swift hunters.

Glossary

dim — not very bright

hatch — to break out of an egg

hunt — to chase and kill animals for food

pectoral fin — the hard, flat limb on either side of a shark

prey — an animal hunted by another animal for food

pup — a young shark

shore — the place where the water meets land; many sharks swim in the shallow water near the shore.

steer — to move in a certain direction

swift — moving or able to move very fast

Read More

Crossingham, John, and Bobbie Kalman. *The Life Cycle of a Shark.* The Life Cycle Series. New York: Crabtree, 2006.

Klein, Adam G. *Mako Sharks.* Sharks. Edina, Minn.: Abdo, 2006.

Lindeen, Carol K. *Sharks.* Under the Sea. Mankato, Minn.: Capstone Press, 2005.

Internet Sites

FactHound offers a safe, fun way to find Internet sites related to this book. All of the sites on FactHound have been researched by our staff.

Here's how:

1. Visit *www.facthound.com*

2. Choose your grade level.

3. Type in this book ID **1429617292** for age-appropriate sites. You may also browse subjects by clicking on letters, or by clicking on pictures and words.

4. Click on the **Fetch It** button.

FactHound will fetch the best sites for you!

Index

Word Count: 123

Grade: 1

Early-Intervention Level: 18